Sing standards.
homemade organic meal tast
juckmuk + urine in litt
Take a class in something of
in (herbology)
study spanish

La Bella Figura

How to Live a Chic, Simple, and European-Style Life

By Kristi Belcamino

Buy beautiful clothes even if you can only afford 1 new
outfit a year.
cultivate small perfect wardrobes you love and wear
everything
perfect comfortable custom clothes
when I only have clothes I love in my closet, I look
better.
Its OK to wear something more then 1x a week
You dont need to wear something new each day of
the week!
"simple isnt easy" book
If it does not make you feel good, donate it.
Know first who you are, then adorn yourself
accordingly.

You should only buy something if you cant
wait to wear it that very night. Trust your
gut instinct.
"Imagin yourself through the eyes of
those who dont know you, as well as those
who adore you. Then of looking your best
as something you do for yourself as
well as for everyone around you."

La Bella Figura

The literal translation of *la bella figura* from Italian means "beautiful figure." From the cradle, little Italian bambinos are raised with the knowledge that presenting *la bella figura* means striving to look and act your best in every situation.

In the book "Lovers" by Judith Krantz, when the heroine, Gigi meets two businessmen she is immediately struck by the care they have taken with their appearance and grooming.

"Their suits, their shirts, their ties, their shoes, their haircuts, even their fingernails were all beyond perfection, if there was such a thing . . .

Bella figura. As the words popped into her mind, she knew instantly that the Collins brothers were Italian by heritage. No American businessman without Italian blood would lavish the time, money and attention that were necessary to look the way they did.

To present *la bella figura* to the world, no matter what was going on inside, was an Italian tradition that reached from the nobility to the peasants."

Of course, you don't have to be an Italian to achieve this — you just have to think like one.

But achieving *la bella figura* is much more than putting time and energy into the image you present through clothes and grooming — it goes much deeper than that.

To Italians, "presenting yourself well in thought, word and deed is a matter of personal dignity," writes Raeleen D'Agostino Mautner in her book, "Living La Dolce Vita."

"The foreign visitor to Italy is typically amazed to observe how polished the men and women of the *bel paese* look, how good they appear to feel about themselves, and how graciously they interact with one another. Italian life is undeniably lived with a constant eye toward aesthetic beauty, dignity and civility. Learning to enhance the body and mind one is born with is more important than having been endowed with genetic perfection," she writes.

To me, an Italian-American mother, *la bella figura* is about looking and acting your best in every situation while savoring the simple things in life, such as family, food, wine, good conversation, books, and movies.

It is about slowing down to appreciate the beauty that is already around you and acknowledging the blessings you already have in your life.

Much of my inspiration is from my European friends who seem to naturally embody these qualities and instinctively live a life focused on these simple pleasures.

There is something about how they live their lives that seems exactly right to me.

"They're likely to judge you on what you've read and not what you have. It's not a consumer culture. It's about honoring time and figuring out how to do more with less and being creative and using your imagination." – Debra Ollivier, author of "Entre Nous" and "What French Women Know."

I hope by reading this book you are able to live a richer, fuller life without having to spend a dollar more to do so. In fact, my goal is to inspire you to live this type of lifestyle — one that involves spending less money, having less stuff, and incurring less stress.

I am sharing some of what has inspired me over the years. I truly believe that there can be art in the way you: dress, eat, act, decorate your home, spend your money, use your leisure time, and look at the world. You can find beauty in everything around you and all that you do.

CHAPTER 1

Living La Dolce Vita

Italians know how to live. They know how to eke every last drop of pleasure out of life — by enjoying a bowl of pistachio gelato, savoring the feel of an ocean breeze, or soaking in the sounds and sights of a night at the opera. They know that the secret to life is in living, not having.

This section is about how to live a life rich in all the things that money can't buy. At the end of your life, what remains are your memories. Not the new car you bought. Not the designer wardrobe in your closet. Not the house full of stuff. As you live your life, try to ensure you will not have any regrets in how you spend the moments of your life because your time *is* your life.

The first thing you need to do to live a life that is in line with *la bella figura* is to stop "buying" and start "doing."

Experiences Instead of Things

For me creating *la bella figura* involves living a life filled with quality over quantity. It is about embracing that "less is more." In essence, it's about valuing experiences over possessions.

This might mean spending your leisure time with friends. For instance, maybe lingering over a cafe au lait at the neighborhood coffee shop instead of meeting that same friend for a shopping excursion at the mall.

It could mean working fewer hours so you have more time to spend with your friends or more time to indulge in your hobbies and passions.

Maybe for you, it means living with that old couch so you can spend money on piano lessons for your children. It might mean using the same dishes and silverware you got as a wedding present twenty years ago and splurging on a membership at the opera instead.

For me, prioritizing how I spend my money and time means happily driving a used vehicle. Rather than buy a new vehicle that will cost me a bundle in monthly car payments — not to mention higher car insurance — I'd rather drive my trusty, paid-off vehicle. As long as it gets me from point A to point B safely and efficiently, I don't care what I drive. I'd rather have more money to spend on an experience. It seems many Europeans agree "Our next vacation means much more to us than a new car and we would never sacrifice the former for the latter except in case of dire necessity. Give us being and feeling over having any day," — Mireille Guiliano of "French Women Don't Get Fat."

Many Europeans have had to be frugal — credit is not as easily obtained in many countries. And let's face it — without credit you can't spend money you don't have. It's very Euro Chic to only spend what you can afford and to save up for something special. I think when you have to save for something you end up appreciating it more. Having less access to credit encourages Europeans to prioritize their spending for maximum satisfaction.

In "C'est La Vie," author Suzy Gershman writes, "People in France made less money than those in the Unites States but still lived better — partly because of this slower pace of life, partly because of the cultural importance of a good meal (with good wine, *bien sur*) and partly because with less discretionary income, priorities were better defined. If a French person had to choose between new clothes or a concert ticket, the ticket usually won out."

This "less is more" approach applies to everything you own: kitchen accouterments, knickknacks, bed linens, dishes, art objects and even clothes! I'll go into this more later.

The Sweet Life – La Dolce Vita

Living *la dolce vita*, which goes hand-in-hand with the *la bella figura* lifestyle, is about taking the time to savor the simple pleasures in life. These small delights are different for everybody. It could be the pleasure of sleeping in on Sunday morning and then spending the next two hours at your favorite café, sipping your cappuccino, and reading the New York Times.

It could be the joy of preparing a gourmet meal and enjoying it with your family or friends. Maybe for you, it is the satisfaction of working with your hands in the garden, planting flowers and vegetables you will enjoy all summer. A few of my passions are photography, books, movies and playing chess. I try to devote time to do at least one of these pleasures a few times a week.

I also find one of the simplest and yet most satisfying pleasures in my life is dining *al fresco* at the picnic table on my patio. I set the table with a cheery, bright colored tablecloth and use my good plates and glasses. (Actually that is another very European concept – using the good stuff and not saving it. I only have the "good" stuff.) Eating outside is a tradition I am establishing for my children. As soon as the warm weather rolls around, they ask me every day if we can eat dinner outside.

Another activity I absolutely love is having friends over for dinner and having good food, wine, and great conversation with lots of laughter involved.

Last summer we had my French friend and her family over. We started with small dishes of antipasti, such as olives and pepperoncini to nibble on. The first course was homemade pesto (made from the basil from my garden) on pasta. The second course was pork chops on the grill with roasted asparagus. And, of course we had wine with dinner. After the pork chops, we had a romaine and avocado salad, a cheese course and then Limoncello with the homemade flourless cake my friend had brought.

The dinner stretched for hours and included bouts of conversation and guitar playing out at the picnic table until it was dark and only the candles illuminated our faces. At the end of the night my French friend took me aside and thanked me, saying how much she enjoyed herself. She mentioned that none of her other American friends had ever served her such a European-style dinner.

Hosting dinner parties like this is one of my simple pleasures in life. So much so that I've made it part of my self-image. I'll explain.

In the book "Style Statement," by Danielle LaPorte and Carrie McCarthy, one exercise the authors suggest to determine your style is to imagine yourself the subject of a celebrity profile in a magazine. Imagining what picture you want to accompany the article is a great way to help distill your style.

I answered the question by saying that I would want to be photographed either at my kitchen table or at the picnic table in my backyard. I would wear a flowered dress. I would be sitting before the remains of a great feast. Friends and family would surround me and my head would be thrown back in laughter. Put food on the table, my family around me, a glass of wine in my hand and that really is me at my happiest. Take time to really think about what makes you happy -- where and when you are your happiest -- and then make sure you are making time to create those moments in your life.

"The Price of Happiness"

An article from the July 2009 issue of Good Housekeeping magazine sums up a lot of my philosophy and views on money and how to live the *bella figura* lifestyle.

The article basically says that you can find joy, happiness and contentment no matter what your income is.

But you have to think carefully about how you spend your money to make this happen.

"The golden rule: Devote your dollars to things that further your goals and beliefs," said one researcher quoted in the article. "It's now very clear that nurturing the things that you value — whether that's becoming more cultured or redesigning your garden — is what makes people happier."

Buying material goods usually only provides temporary happiness and when you set your sights on acquisition, you often only gain the feeling of wanting more.

"Purchases that support your own values, however, are more satisfying because they help to boost your feelings of self-worth," said the article. *writing classes* *vocabulary book* *crosswords*

To "get the most bliss for your buck" you have to think long and hard before you spend your money. The article recommends investing in experiences rather than belongings: "One of the best ways to invest in happiness is to focus on doing rather than owning … 57 percent (of people asked) said they got more happiness from things they had done — taking a vacation, riding a bike, strolling through a museum, eating a pretzel with a friend — than from stuff they had bought." It's not only that these activities are fun while we are doing them; it is that we are creating long-lasting memories. One mother of two interviewed in the article said she has made her financial priorities so they will equal good memories.

"She isn't interested in replacing the television she bought in 1988," the article says. "Instead, she saves her money so she can buy airplane tickets and travel to new places. The jaunts, *Fatima Hawaii* she says, are exciting stress relievers — even well after they're over and she's back at work: 'I recently spent five days in Paris with my husband, walking down old streets steeped in history. Thinking back on that during an otherwise difficult day relaxes me.' "

These memories will bring her happiness for years to come. "Material things, on the other hand, quickly lose their luster," this article states. "You may spend hours fantasizing about buying a silk scarf, several days shopping for it and perhaps even some time enjoying it, but not much. Your brain quickly adjusts to the fact that the scarf is folded in your drawer, and before long, you're so used to its being there, you can barely remember when it wasn't.

"Once the object of your obsession, now the scarf blends into the background and becomes as normal to you as hot water, Internet access or automatic-drip coffee."

The article recommends people splurge on mini treats. "It may sound counterintuitive, but researchers have found that over time that small, inexpensive indulgences have virtually the same emotional impact as big, pricey ones — making the little things a much better buy."

Another study examined the purchase of big items versus small ones and the happiness quotient.

"It was the frequent treats of chocolate bars or bottles of wine with takeout dinners that made both groups happy — not the pricier purchase of artwork, designer luggage or CD players."

homemade organic!

"Voluntary Simplicity as Hedonism"

I also love this article by Philip Brewer that was found on one of my favorite money websites, www.wisebread.com.

"When people talk about voluntary simplicity (or living a frugal lifestyle under any of its many names), they often do so in terms of deprivation. The descriptions are all about doing without stuff. To me, that's completely wrong. Voluntary simplicity is fundamentally a hedonistic lifestyle.

"What do hedonists do? They do what ordinary people seem only to do when they're on vacation. They go places that are interesting or beautiful and they linger in them. They go dancing and go to parties. They read good books. They hang out with cool people. They hike in the mountains and swim in the ocean and go sailing. They play golf or tennis. They eat good food and drink good wine. They listen to music or play music. They go to museums and theaters. They do whatever gives them pleasure until they're tired, and then they lie in the shade and take a nap.

"To me, voluntary simplicity is exactly the same thing. You think about what gives you the most pleasure and then arrange your life so you can do exactly that.

"I saw a poster once that said, "My tastes are simple: I like to have the best." It's a sentiment that probably resonates with everyone. But you can't have the best of everything–where would you keep it? So, you have the best of only a few things, the things that matter the most to you. And, if you get rid of the other stuff–stuff that doesn't matter as much to you–then your whole life gets easier. With less stuff you can live in a smaller house, or an apartment instead of a house, or a smaller apartment.

"But a small apartment doesn't mean a small life. A small apartment is a means to an end. The end is a life doing whatever you want."

I love these two articles and that is why I reproduced them almost word-for-word. They are so inspirational that I re-read them frequently.

12 Easy Things to Do to Enjoy *La Dolce Vita*

1.   Dine *al fresco* whenever you have the chance. Even if you live in an apartment in a big city, have a picnic at the park, eat at a sidewalk café or if you have a rooftop, you can have a picnic on a blanket with votive candles. If you have a small balcony, invest in a café table and chairs and wait until dark to light some candles and eat, admiring the city lights. If you have a backyard, carve out a small area for a picnic or bistro table and set a table with real dishes and linens each night.

2.   Turn off the TV. Go for a walk, listen to music, take a bath, play cards, read a book, take pictures, polish your toenails, make art, write a letter, make love, garden, write ~~poetry~~ screenplay, eat ice cream, daydream.

goal 3.   Walk. If you can, walk as often as possible instead of driving. It is good exercise, but also puts you in touch with the world around you in a meaningful way.

4.   Learn to prepare one fantastically delicious meal that makes you happy to make and to eat.

5.   Use cloth napkins and set a table every meal, even if you are dining alone.

6.   Eat slowly and savor the taste of your food.

7.   Don't schedule every minute of your life. Give yourself time to nap, read a book or stare at the clouds.

8.   Take a class in something you are interested in: stained glass, yoga, cooking, you name it.

9.   Study a foreign language, even if you already are bilingual.

10.   Find your passions: be it French history, cooking, sculpture or roller-skating and devote meaningful time to it each week _singing_

11.   Have people over for dinner. I learned living in a 300-square-foot studio apartment in Oakland that it doesn't matter how big your place is or how good a cook you are, you can still host a dinner party where people enjoy themselves so much that you have to ask them to leave at 4 a.m. so you can go to bed. Invite people to dine with you, even if you are just having soup. Add some wine, fresh bread, break out the stories, guitar or playing cards and enjoy each other's company.

12.   Buy beautiful clothes, even – especially -- if you can only afford to purchase one new outfit each year.

CHAPTER 2

Creating a Chic, Simple, Perfect Wardrobe

As I mentioned in the beginning of this book, creating *la bella figura* means presenting your best face to the world, in actions and appearance.

It does not take a lot of money to do this. In fact, it shouldn't take any more than you already spend. It is a matter of selection and being picky.

If you are not happy with your clothes or your style and want to improve your *la bella figura*, I am going to hazard a wild guess that maybe, just maybe, you have too many clothes in your closet. After years of studying wardrobe and stylebooks, I truly believe the key to having style is having fewer clothes. If you look at Europeans, for the most part the average woman (not the models or socialites or fashion mavens) have a smaller number of clothes than most Americans.

Stylish French architect Andrée Putman once said, "I love America, and I love American women. But there is one thing that deeply shocks me – American closets. I cannot believe one can dress well when one has so much."

Quality over Quantity

We American women tend to go overboard clothes shopping. Conversely, European women do not. They also do not feel the need to wear a new outfit for each day of the week. Europeans, instead, invest in quality and wear their "good clothes" over and over again. In his book "Freakin' Fabulous," Clinton Kelly observed how the French did this shamelessly.

"… by the time Friday rolled around people were wearing the same outfits they wore on Monday! … They cared more about quality than quantity … they actually paid more for clothes that fit them well and wore them more often."

If you notice, in most French or Italian movies, the characters will be dressed in the same outfit in different scenes that take place on different days.

In the movie "Happily Ever After" the stylish Charlotte Gainsbourg wore the same tweed slacks, silk blouse and dark cardigan in several scenes over several days. Observation of my European friends has shown this is true to life. Europeans wear outfits repeatedly with style and flair.

In my all-time favorite style book, "Simple Isn't Easy" the authors Amy Fine Collins and Olivia Goldsmith quote Manolo Blahnik saying, "It is a question of selection, to choose less. That is something that Americans do not understand. They think that more is better."

Euro Style

One thing I have always admired about European women is their ability to make do. They make do with tiny little apartments. They make do by whipping up a delicious dinner from what they find in their pantries. They make do by cultivating small perfect wardrobes where they love everything and wear everything.

Somehow they are able – with a small number of clothes – to look chic, stylish and unique in every situation.

I noticed this with my Spanish, Greek and German friends in college.

After college I lived in Los Angeles in a big house with several roommates. One of them, from Copenhagen, was incredibly sophisticated and stylish and became a close friend. She had lived in Paris and oozed European chic.

When I met her she was visiting America but then moved in with us and decided to stay for a few years.

When she arrived, she had a large backpack with all of her belongings. All her clothes fit into it, along with any other personal items she brought.

Although, this was some 20 years ago, I remember some of the clothes she pulled out of that backpack:

* A black turtleneck

* Black ballet flats

* Black opaque tights

* Jeans

* A red small print flowered miniskirt

These are the only items I remember, but I do remember that she did not have a whole lot more than that. She bought a few items while she lived with us, but considering she stayed in America for two years, she bought very little to supplement a backpack full of clothes.

She didn't have a lot of clothes or a lot of money, but she always looked chic.

One of my favorite outfits she wore was a pair of Levis, a little baggy on her slim frame, with a man's shirt. The shirt was borrowed from a male friend who had a slight build. It was a short-sleeve brown button-up linen shirt with cream embroidery on the front – sort of a Mexican style shirt. She looked fabulous.

I also remember she often wore her black cashmere turtleneck sweater and a Patty Hearst style beat-up black leather blazer jacket. Once she lost her sweater and was distraught until she could locate it again. I remember thinking to myself how odd that she was so upset over a sweater – why didn't she just go buy another one. I didn't get it at the time. I was thinking like a typical mass consumer in America. Now, with hindsight, I realize that cashmere sweater was not purchased for her to throw away or toss in a corner after a few months. It was probably THE perfect sweater that she had picked out very carefully and thoughtfully and intended to wear faithfully and often for years to come.

Part of her style was her attitude, but part of it was her innate ability to make whatever clothes she had look chic spending barely any money.

A few years later I went to Europe myself for several months and saw European chic in person. I have since been on a quest to achieve this effortless chic, keeping my closet small but filled with perfect items.

When you only have a few carefully selected items in your closet that all look good on you, then you are on your way to achieving lifelong style.

I know that when I only have clothes I love in my closet, I look better.

But most of us don't have that perfect wardrobe. We have mistakes we have bought, either on sale, or on a whim, or clothes that just don't mesh with other items in our closet.

So your first step in creating a perfect wardrobe needs to involve casting a critical eye on your current clothes before you even think about buying any new ones.

The Purge/Closet Clean Out

I always recommend starting from scratch if your wardrobe isn't working. It is better to own one perfect fitting skirt than a bunch of unflattering ones. Find that one perfect skirt, or pair of jeans or dress pants (depending on what you wear the most) and then slowly build your closet from there.

custom

Here is what I have gleaned in the many books and articles I've read on evaluating your wardrobe. I try to follow these rules and revisit them often:

When it comes to purging your closet, here are some criteria that can help you decide what goes and what stays.

* Get rid of anything that you haven't worn in a year. There have been a few exceptions to this, including a velvet vintage cape that I only wear occasionally to a company Christmas party or other special event. So I may go more than a year without wearing it, but it is worth keeping because it is so unique and lovely.

* Get rid of anything that you don't love. If it doesn't make you feel good, ditch it. Out. Why keep something if it just makes you feel so-so or is adequate or you think fills a void. If you don't love it, get rid of it. Life is too short to wear something you don't like.

* Get rid of anything that doesn't really fit. It is either too big or too small. Either way, you should love yourself enough to buy clothes that fit. So what if you do lose weight? Wonderful! You then deserve to buy new clothes in your new size. Even if you can only afford to buy one fabulous dress in your new size that you can wear three times a week. Clothing stores are always going to be there. You can always slowly re-build your wardrobe if you lose weight and need new clothes. Remember less is more. Get over the idea that you need to have something different to wear each day of the week. It is okay to wear the same item more than once a week.

* Get rid of anything that is ratty, torn or needs to be repaired. If it looks sloppy and that is not the look you are going for, then dump it. If it needs mending or tailoring or repairing (such as a broken sandal strap) either fix it or toss it.

The "Simple Isn't Easy" authors give the perfect blueprint for closet purging that I will paraphrase below, adding my own tips. (By the way, if you don't own this book, go get it. It will give you great ideas for closet purging and finding style. It was my style bible for years and I would not part with my dog-eared copy for anything!)

1.   Try on all your clothes. Using the criteria above, sort them into two piles: The keep (yes) and the toss (no) pile. Be very, very picky here. Unless you "love" it, put it in the "no" pile. Don't worry it will not be tossed or given away until you know for sure that it is wrong for you.

2.   Figure out what looks best on you by what remains in your "yes" pile. Is it tailored slacks, camisoles and blazers or is it flowing dresses paired with cowboy boots? (I'll talk more about finding your uniform or your style in a minute.)

3.   Take another look at the "no" pile. Try on these clothing items one more time, using the criteria I mentioned above: Do you love it? Does it fit? Is it in good shape? "Simple Isn't Easy" author Olivia Goldsmith wrote that it doesn't matter if it was Versace and the most expensive skirt you ever bought, if it doesn't look good on you, get rid of it. Based on this advice, I actually had a sleek black Armani skirt I finally parted with because it just didn't look right on me no matter how much I wanted it to look good.

4.   Look at the "yes" pile again. At this point, you shouldn't have ten pairs of gray slacks, but you might have one pair that fits you perfectly, flattering every curve. Do you have tops to wear with it? Start a "needs" shopping list: gray slacks - need matching tops.

Maybe when you have done your closet purge, you only have one dress and four tops that remain. That is okay. You can slowly piece-by-piece rebuild your wardrobe so it is perfect. I'll get to that later. Don't be afraid to have a bare closet. You are starting from scratch to create your own small, perfect wardrobe and sometimes that takes drastic measures.

Test Drive

After your closet purge, Fine Collins and Goldsmith say don't throw or give away anything at first. Set them aside for a while you test drive your new wardrobe for a few weeks. I find this helpful. I put clothes in the donation box in my basement. Usually my favorite charity picks up on my street once every few months, so the clothes can end up sitting there for a while. Once or twice I have fished something out of the basement box and worn it, though very rarely. I have never regretted purging my closet of anything ever.

Anne Barone, the uber chic author of the "Chic & Slim" series of books talks about how she once thought she had made a mistake when she got rid of a jacket during a closet purge. However, it accidentally escaped the donation box and when she found it in a closet she tried it on again. When she did, she realized her initial impulse in donating it was right.

Only Buy What You Love

"Women usually love what they buy, yet hate two-thirds of what is in their closets." ~Mignon McLaughlin, The Neurotic's Notebook, 1960

Now this part is important: make sure you don't repeat your mistakes and buy the wrong things over and over.

You may find after your closet purge that you are missing many basics. I want you to analyze your style and body type very carefully and come up with a list of the very basics you will need to have a working wardrobe. You can always add to these items later. I'll talk more about finding your style and shopping below. But meanwhile, here is what the "Simple Isn't Easy" authors say you should memorize to keep stylish.

"Mantra 1: I want to look stylish. To do it, I must keep things simple.

Mantra 2: A full closet does not mean stylish.

Mantra 3: Shopping all the time does not mean stylish.

Mantra 4: Changing my look every season (or month, or week or day!) does not mean stylish."

Here's what Nancy Marie, the author of "Style, Beauty, Trimness" has to say about only owning what you love:

"Excess is rarely the best approach towards elegance," she writes. "Why do we think we need so much? Many women have tons of clothes but 'have nothing to wear.' Pare down to the basics. Have a love affair with your clothes! If you love everything in your closet, you will radiate the confidence that comes from being dressed in an outfit that makes you feel fantastic. Own nothing unattractive. If it does not fit, is ugly or simply does not make you feel good: donate it. "If you own nothing unattractive, you will never have to worry about looking anything less than good."

Finding your Style

"Know, first, who you are; and then adorn yourself accordingly." ~Epictetus

So how exactly do you find your style? It takes a critical eye and a lot of study and analysis. A lot of it has to do with your gut instinct. I truly believe that when you try on a new clothing item and look at yourself in the mirror, if you don't IMMEDIATELY like what you see then it's not working. The best advice I ever heard was that you should only buy something if you can't wait to wear it that very night. That little gem alone has saved me hundreds of dollars on clothes. Trust your gut instinct. It is usually right. What happens, though, is we start to over think things and our logical mind works hard to override what our instinct is telling us.

Our initial reaction might be, "You know that color white just makes me look like the walking dead." But then your logical mind will say, "But I really love the look of white on a hot summer day. Remember how cool and crisp Sophie looked in that white blouse the other day at the dinner party? I want to look like that, she is so chic." So your mind will always try to justify and override your heart or gut or whatever you call it (and this goes for much more in life than just those times you are analyzing your wardrobe). So my rule of thumb is unless I feel GREAT, not just okay, in a clothing item, I get rid of it, or I don't buy it. Okay is not good enough.

I just read a book that gave me a simple way to refine/define my style. "French Style" by Veronique Vienne is out of print and goes for about $100 on Amazon. Luckily, I was able to get it at my library and copied down practically every word in my little leather journal. Now I can frequently refer to Vienne's words of wisdom until I save up money to have my own treasured copy. I'll share the highlights with you here:

The most valuable advice in the book for me was when Vienne suggested readers use this exercise to discover their style:

"The following will help you see yourself in the way others see you: Imagine walking down the street: the choice of a silhouette is your most important decision. Determine how you want to look from a distance. Ask yourself: who is this elegant woman coming toward me — and what is she wearing? A roomy jacket with slim pants? A sinuous and flowing dress? A tailored and slick suit? Trust that first impression it defines you."

Without a second's hesitation, I saw myself dressed just as Julie Delpy in "Before Sunset" as she is walking down the street in perfect fitting jeans, a soft, feminine gorgeous blouse, heels and a jacket slung over her bag. She had slightly messy hair and was casual, yet chic, sexy, nonchalant and effortless looking. Bingo.

That is my style and what I aim for every day.

Please try this exercise. It worked better for me than I could ever have imagined in finding my own style.

Here are a few more tips from Vienne's book:

French Style

• "To dress like a French Woman, don't try to look like a model – try to be a role model. Think of the next generation; give them something to aspire to. Try to imagine yourself through the eyes of those who don't know you, as well as those who adore you. Think of looking your best as something you do for your own sake and for the sake of everyone around you …"

• "Fashion is a language. Use it to communicate your intentions. Present a consistent image. Don't change your style all the time. Take a lesson from men. Wear the same type of outfit all week long and select accessories that are unmistakably yours."

- "To dress with flair, the French woman reads all about it in fashion magazines — and then forgets it all. But beware. There is a difference between ignoring fashion altogether and choosing to disregard it. It's the difference between cool and boring, crisp and bland, polished and dull. Remind yourself that you've got nothing to wear, but don't dress negligently. Eliminate superfluous and excessive detail. Get rid of the pretension. Simplify …"

- "Unlike the American woman who loves to save money, the French woman loves to spend it, but sparingly. She compares value, not price, and calls any purchase that delivers what it promises a bargain. She gets as much pleasure dropping some change on a cheap-and-chic necklace as she gets splurging on a costly luxury. Money well spent is money that buys a sense of worth. The more expensive items test her self-esteem more than her sense of style."

- "She reviews the contents of her closet and makes a wish list – but leaves the list on the kitchen table. If you can't remember what you wrote down, you probably don't need it." I love Veronique Vienne! She also has many other great books you should check out.

Uniform

"Style comes from finding a uniform that feels effortless and comfortable and then sticking to it." – Charlotte Gainsbourg

I like the idea of a uniform as a way to help solidify your style. When I say uniform, I mean a way of dressing that is uniquely yours and works for your body type, personality and lifestyle. My adorable sister-in-law is a feisty, outspoken redhead with more personality than the French Quarter during Mardi gras. She has a very distinct style that suits her to a tee.

Every single day of her life, she dresses or skirts with either high heel boots or high-heel sandals. (No flats for this preschool teacher who has 4-year-old girls swooning over her pastel pink and rhinestone pumps.) She also wears lots of brooches, necklaces, bracelets or earrings in beautiful colors. Yes ?

(Not all at once). And her outfits are almost always colorful and color coordinated. For example, one night we went to a fancy dinner and she wore a poufy purple and olive green silky skirt, olive green tights, high-heeled, deep purple Mary Jane's, with a soft cashmere olive green scarf knotted at her throat and pinned with an antique purple and green jeweled brooch.

Her look is consistent and she always looks stylish. She has her uniform down to a science; she even wears skirts (casual ones) when we go camping. Everyone knows and recognizes her style as uniquely hers and one that suits her personality, lifestyle, and body shape.

Color Palette

One of the easiest ways to create a chic, simple and timeless wardrobe is to restrict the colors in your closet to no more than five colors that all work together. This can vary for different seasons. For instance, below you will see how my winter colors differ slightly from my summer ones. But first, let's look at how to pick your five colors. I base this on advice I read from Jennifer Skinner of http://jenniferskinner.blogspot.com. She used to have a "Wardrobe Planning Website" with information on picking wardrobe colors. I'm sad she no longer has that site and doesn't blog anymore. She is so smart about clothes! Anyway, this is based on what I learned from her ideas:

1.   Pick your basic neutral color. Pick the neutral that flatters you the most. You probably already instinctively know what neutral suits you best, but sometimes we get caught up in the appeal of black. If you are unsure, I would ask the advice of several people you know. You can even go to a high-end clothing store and model the different neutrals for the salesclerks, asking their opinions. When picking your neutral, be sure to pick something you can find and coordinate year after year. I would one of the following: black, brown, beige, *camel*

navy or gray.

2.   Next, pick some version of white. No matter what your coloring is, you can find a white, cream, ivory or bisque, *?*

which flatters you.

Turquoise Purple
magenta Red Black? love
pink

3.   Then pick three other colors. I suggest you try to find

three colors that will coordinate with your neutral color. Make

one of these colors your signature color – that one color that

you love, love, love. You know the one I'm talking about --

that one color that garners compliments every time you wear

it. You might have to think about it if you haven't worn it for a

while, but you remember what color you wear that lights up

your face and that everyone comments on.

There are so many books about determining your colors, not

to mention professionals and websites that will help you do

this.

I remember reading that French women are sometimes

advised to never wear more than three colors at a time, as

well. This just makes sense to me.

Of course, my sister-in-law, who I mentioned above, is the

perfect example of someone who does a terrific job breaking

this rule. So, obviously it doesn't apply to everyone. It works

for me, though.

A long time ago, I read on a Yahoo group about a chic French woman who restricted her wardrobe colors to black, white and red. Period. She also wore the colors in prints, such as stripes and checks. She added some spice to her clothes with scarves in bright colors, but her actual clothing colors never varied. As she got older, she planned on transforming this palette so it was softer: gray, cream and pink, I believe. That is discipline. I'm sure it made getting dressed easier because everything coordinated and it definitely gave her a recognizable style that was all her own.

So if you want to look chic, one easy way to do so is to restrict your color palette.

Look Book

This is a place, either in your computer file or in a folder or binder, where you keep pictures of people who inspire you, looks you like, fabrics you love, clothes you want to buy, articles on style and so on.

I keep an electronic folder on my laptop that is filled with pictures of celebrities who inspire me (style icons - see below) and outfits and clothing items I like.

In addition, I have a three-ring binder that is filled with plastic sheet covers. I put inspirational pictures in these covers. Pictures I have ripped out of magazines of outfits I like, haircuts I want, shoes I covet and articles about living *la bella figura* or the European lifestyle. Anything that motivates or inspires me goes in this binder or my electronic folder.

Style Icons

In determining your own style, it helps to look to others to determine what looks you like. It really helps to find someone who is even a little bit similar to you in looks.

Look around in magazines, online or even in your town and find a style icon that inspires you. Don't try to copy this woman's look, but use it as a launching pad for creating your own unique style.

Shopping

I always keep two lists in my little leather journal. One is a "needs" list and one is a "wants" list.

For instance, your needs list might include basics, such as black wool tights, a black cardigan and some black sandals. Your wants list might have items such as vintage cowboy boots and luxurious silk pajamas.

Needs are the basics that will get you through the seasons. Wants are the ones that will add a little spice and style to your wardrobe.

When I shop, unless I know immediately that it is exactly what I've been looking for, I also try to wait a day or a few hours after I try it on before I buy it. I may ask the clerk to hold it and then go get lunch or a coffee to make sure I still want it as badly once I am away from it. This has saved me a lot of money over the years.

But let's back up a minute and go back into the dressing room. Here's where you should have your moment of clarity. If you try it on and your response is anything less than an ecstatic, enthusiastic "YES!!!!!" – The kind where you are grinning in the mirror and spinning around happy as can be, then go get a coffee. Go think on it. Or better yet, skip it altogether. Why would you spend your hard-earned money on anything that doesn't make you feel like a million bucks?

Thrift Stores/Garage Sales/Consignment Shops

For the most part, my thrift store or consignment store shopping is more to find items that might be on my "wants" list. These are the items that add the spice and style to my wardrobe. I may look for that black cardigan at the thrift store, but usually my "needs" are bought new. They are my basics, the foundations of my wardrobe.

For instance, I always skip the jeans or pants section at my neighborhood thrift store because I always buy these items new. Jeans are a staple of my wardrobe and I will spend a bit more on them. Plus, experience has taught me, this is one area I don't find what I want thrift shopping because I am so specific about the jeans I want.

When I am thrifting, I look at blouses, tops, sweaters, skirts, dresses, scarves and shoes. What simplifies the thrift store hunt for me and makes it work is my limited color palette. Once you have narrowed your wardrobe down to five colors, thrift store shopping is a breeze. With the discipline to only look at items in these five colors, you have a better chance of not getting frustrated during the hunt.

If I have extra time, I cruise through the coats and jackets section looking for something unique and/or vintage, like the Tommy Bahamas trench coat I found thrifting. Today, as I write this, is Black Friday. I went to the thrift store and found a gorgeous Eileen Fisher charcoal gray sweater with the price tags still attached for $19.

As you make your way through the aisles and something catches your eye, do a quick touch. I can easily tell if something is high quality just by feeling it. Sometimes the beauty of buying something that has already been worn is you can see how well it holds up. If a sweater is going to pill, it usually will have done so by the time it hits the thrift store. Or if a shirt is going to be unbearably difficult to keep ironed, you should be able to tell right away.

When you are looking for second-hand or vintage items, don't forget garage sales. I've had great luck at them the past few years.

Must-Have List

Here is my own personal Top 10 List every stylish woman should have in her wardrobe. These are those basics I was talking about that are the foundation of a stylish wardrobe. Many of you have seen dozens of these lists over the years, so I won't expand or linger on it too much.

My list of wardrobe must haves:

1.   *Custom* Jeans that fit you perfectly. I think women at every age from 18 to 80 can look great in jeans. It just takes a lot of work to find which ones work for you and your figure and lifestyle. For me, a stay-at-home, work-at-home mother, Levis are my main staple. It took a lot of trial and error to find the right jeans that are the most flattering to my shape. Luckily, Levis are inexpensive! I am starting to really like black jeans for a slightly dressier look.

2.   Skirt in your main neutral color, pencil or in my case A-line. This could be denim, wool, jersey, etc. If you don't like skirts, then instead pick a pair of dressier pants that flatter you in a neutral color. They could even be dressier jeans if that is your staple and you love denim, just pick something a little nicer to wear for out to dinner or for more dressy events when you want to look a little more dressed up.

3.   Trench Coat. I truly believe that this is a timeless, stylish item that every woman should own. It can be the iconic Catherine Deneuve beige, or it can be black or even bright pink or red. It can be belted or an unbelted style. A trench just screams stylish to me.

4.   Jacket. I have two blazers: one in black wool and navy velvet. You may want one that is in a jean material or silk or tweed. Maybe your style is best suited by wearing a Chanel style jacket. With a jacket like this you can always add a little extra personal style to a dress, skirt or jeans.

5.	Cardigan or pullover sweater in a neutral color that matches everything you own. I love deep V-neck cashmere sweaters.

6.	Classic pumps in your main neutral color. I find super classic pumps a tad boring so I currently have a pair of black patent leather Mary Jane pumps.

7.	Knee-high leather boots to wear with skirts in winter or colder days. I know some women say it is difficult to find knee-high boots that fit them well, so it might take a little work to find the right pair for you, but they really do look stylish and work so well in colder climates during the winter.

8. ~~Flat~~ *Roomy* Ankle boots *Goal* to wear with pants and jeans.

9.	Some type of signature earrings: pearls, diamond studs, in my case, I wear silver ~~hoop earrings.~~ Maybe your signature is to wear giant costume jewelry earrings every day. Just pick your look and stick with it.

10. A Little Black Dress. I just don't believe people who say you don't need this. Everyone needs this. Everyone can find a style that suits him or her. This is the most versatile, stylish thing you can own.

To these basics, all you need to add is some tops or blouses in a style, cut and color that suits you, some accessories such as belts, scarves, and jewelry and you will be on your way to a very chic, simple and timeless wardrobe.

Lingerie

Just like everything else I've said about clothes, when it comes to lingerie, less is more. Ditch all your ugly bras and panties and invest in something pretty and comfortable.

Try Aubade, Lise Charmel, Simone Perele, Chantelle, La Perla. For the budget conscious, Victoria's Secret has some nice items. Some of these bra sets are expensive, so maybe you just need one black bra and one beige and replace them every six months or so.

I don't have a drawer full of lingerie. I have a select few beautiful items in basic colors along with a few take-my-breath-away beautiful ones. They are all of the highest quality I can afford and I baby them so I can keep them looking nice for as long as possible.

Which reminds me: Baby all your clothes. Don't throw them on the floor at night. If they need to be washed, put them in the hamper or whatever. If they don't, immediately hang them up so they don't wrinkle or get dirty. I wash my clothes in cold water and hang them dry. Taking care of your clothes helps you maintain *la bella figura*, but you can also find a certain amount of pleasure in caring for the things you own.

CHAPTER 3

Mangia! Mangia!

The Pleasures of Food

Italians know that sitting down to a good meal is by far one of the most pleasurable experiences in life. Italians, like the French, usually eat their largest meal in the afternoon and linger over it for hours before returning to work.

After work the Italians take an evening walk through the piazza (village square) before eating a light dinner. This leisurely social walk is called *la passeggiata.*

Watching this stroll from the sidelines is like attending a mini fashion show. Men, women and children are dressed up. They didn't first go home from work and change into their sweatpants and sneakers. Even the men and women who are retired get dressed up for the evening *la passeggiata.*

Older men who may not actually stroll might sit at outdoor café tables and watch the show, sipping espresso and playing cards.

Much of family life and community life is centered on food and the rituals surrounding it, such as the pre-dinner la passeggiata.

For Italians, food is much more than just nourishment or fuel for the body. Cooking someone a great meal is also considered a labor of love. It is a way to spend quality time with the people in your life.

The Big Sunday Dinner

Italians love to eat al fresco. Picture for a moment the most romantic image of Italians eating their Big Sunday Dinner: They are seated on a patio outside a big stone Tuscan farmhouse overlooking olive groves and grape vines.

More than a dozen people are seated at a rustic wooden table covered with bright pottery, heaping bowls of pasta with a red sauce, platters of meats, plates of cooked green vegetables, baskets of fresh fruit, hunks of freshly baked bread loaves, sparkling water carafes and bottles of wine.

Dinner involves lots of laughter and conversation and a bit of teasing among the diners. After a few hours, the meal is over, but the family is still conversing and relaxing at the table. Dark-haired children chase each other around the table as the adults linger, peeling and placing slices of fruit in their wine glasses as the sun begins to dip toward the horizon.

The Big Sunday Dinner is centered on food, but it is about way more than that. It is about taking the time to enjoy the people in your life and share yourself with them.

Many Italian-Americans, including me, continue this tradition from their homeland by indulging in the Big Sunday Dinner. Eating meals together is one of the most important traditions I am working to maintain in my own family.

Studies show that teens that come from homes that eat meals together are less likely to drink, smoke, do drugs, be depressed, have eating disorders or contemplate suicide. These teens are also more likely to eat healthier foods, have higher test scores and wait to have sex.

A National Merit Scholarship Corporation survey found that the common factor in all its scholars over the past 20 years was this: all of the kids had come from families who sat down to dinner together at least three nights a week.

Shattering Stereotypes

Despite the image of the chubby, 4-foot-tall, dressed in black, Italian grandmother, Italians have fewer problems with obesity than Americans.

(According to a 1998 article in Fortune Magazine, 24.9 percent of American women struggle with obesity. In comparison, only 6.3 percent of Italian women were considered obese.)

Living a bella figura lifestyle means enjoying food but not overindulging. It also means choosing foods that are close to their most natural state, not overly processed concoctions.

Eat Like a European

My eating habits are dictated by a few books I've read over the years: "The Fat Fallacy: Applying the French Diet to the American Lifestyle," by Will Clower; "French Women Don't Get Fat," by Mireille Guiliano; all of Anne Barone's "Chic and Slim" books; and "In Defense of Food," by Michael Pollan. From these books I created some guidelines on how and what I eat to make myself a more mindful eater.

– Only eat while seated

This means if I am at a party or event, I make a plate and go sit down to eat it. I don't stand at the counter or bar and graze on chips and dip or whatever.

– Put utensils down between bites

This slows me down.

– Take small bites. Chew thoroughly. Savor each bite.

I get more pleasure from eating this way. I also realize I am satisfied sooner than if I rush through my meal.

– Only eat food you love.

If it doesn't taste awesome to you, don't eat it.

-Keep portions small.

Learn what a true portion size is and try to stick with that. A portion of any type of meat should be about the size of a deck of cards or your palm.

– No snacking.

In addition to these eating habits, I also walk daily during the warmer months.

They sound so simple and they are. But these rules are very effective. It is only when I break them that I gain weight.

What to eat?

I am going to refer to Michael Pollan's excellent 7 food rules. I also recommend buying all of his other books if you are interested in this subject. They are fantastic.

But first, if you are going to remember anything from Pollan, remember his basic rule of thumb for eating:

"Eat food, not too much, mostly plants."

Here are a few of his other rules:

-       Don't eat anything your great grandmother wouldn't recognize as food.

-       Don't eat anything with more than five ingredients, or ingredients you can't pronounce.

- Stay out of the middle of the supermarket; shop on the perimeter of the store.
- Don't eat anything that won't eventually rot. (Pollan says, accurately, that things like Twinkies are not food.)
- It is not just what you eat but how you eat. Stop eating before you are full.

Ban Fake Foods

In our house, I try to avoid processed foods and ban foods with high fructose corn syrup.

It costs more to eat this way, but part of living *la bella figura* means putting your money where it counts — toward your values. One of my core values is raising healthy children so I don't feel guilty when I put my money toward healthy foods for their growing bodies.

Unfortunately, I am not able to do this all the time for everything. For instance, I am a firm believer in organic milk, but can't afford to buy it every shopping trip, so my compromise is that I buy organic milk every other time I go shopping.

Pantry list

Keep a typed grocery list on your refrigerator with the items you use each week. You can print out new copies each week and then circle the items you need to buy. My list is broken down into two sections: staples for my pantry that need to be replaced when they are gone (nonperishables) and items that need to be bought each week (perishables). I circle items when I notice I am running out or when I am menu planning.

Menu Structure/Recipe Book

I love to cook. However, I am not the type of cook who wings it, adding a dash of this or that and knowing it will turn out okay. I really didn't get in touch with my "domestic" side until I was in my thirties; so this may have something to do with not having the confidence to just "throw something together."

I usually strictly adhere to recipes and rarely deviate from them. I have what I call my "repertoire" of recipes I turn to and don't add a new recipe until it is tried and true. I keep all my recipes in plastic sheets in a three-ring notebook. It also has family recipes. I would definitely grab this book in a fire. The recipes I want to try, or that have not been "proven," I keep in the inside pockets of the notebook.

The notebook is divided into several sections: pasta (hey, I am Italian American, so it needs its own section); meat; poultry; miscellaneous (which includes desserts, breads, vinaigrettes, vegetables).

I also have a weekly menu structure I loosely follow:

Sunday: Nine times out of 10 we have the Big Sunday Dinner, which includes pasta (usually spaghetti) with meatballs, Italian sausage, pork chops or all three. I always have fresh baked bread, a green salad, some type of vegetable and dessert.

Monday: Usually after a heavy Sunday meal, we have soup (winter) or salad (summer) on this day or else we have leftovers.

Tuesday: This is often a leftover night or we have eggs and toast.

Wednesday: Pasta night, usually a pasta without a red sauce.

Thursday: Chicken in some form. In the winter this often is a roasted chicken.

Friday: This night is often pizza night, but sometimes we have leftover chicken in some form.

Saturday: This is a "meat" night. I often like to cook pork on this night.

This is a loose structure that helps me decide what to cook each night. I don't always follow it, but it sure helps to wake up in the morning and say, Oh, today is pasta day and so I know what I'm going to make.

Signature Dishes

I find it helpful to have a few tried and true dishes I can whip up either for my family or for company and have complete confidence they will turn out great.

I have my signature salad I always make (romaine lettuce with mashed avocado and homemade honey-mustard vinaigrette); a pasta recipe I received from my sister-in-law and a few other dishes.

So go ahead and practice a few solid recipes until they are perfect and you can pull them out in a pinch. Here are a few of my "signature" dishes.

Recipes

Appetizers

Date and Blue Cheese Bruschetta

1 loaf French bread, sliced into ½ inch slices

Extra virgin olive oil

Kosher salt

Pepper

8 oz. blue cheese

12 dates cut in half with pits removed

4 oz. prosciutto

Preheat oven to 350 degrees. Brush both sides of bread slices with olive oil and put on a baking sheet. Bake for 5 minutes. Flip and bake for 5 minutes more. Remove from oven. Turn broiler to high. Season bread with salt and pepper. Spoon just enough blue cheese to cover bread. Place ½ a date on each slice. Broil 1-2 minutes until cheese melts and date begins to caramelize. Remove and layer with piece of prosciutto. Serve immediately.

Roasted Asparagus and Eggs

Ingredients: 1 bunch medium thick asparagus with tough ends removed, 2 tablespoons olive oil, 1/2 cup balsamic vinegar, 1 teaspoon light brown sugar, 1 tablespoon cider vinegar, 4 large eggs, 2 ounces shaved Parmesan

1. Preheat the oven to 400 degrees. On a baking sheet with a rim, toss asparagus with oil. Season with salt. Bake until asparagus is lightly browned and tender, 15 to 18 minutes (timing will vary depending on thickness of asparagus)

2. In a small saucepan, cook balsamic vinegar and sugar over medium-high heat until syrupy and reduced to 3 tablespoons, about 6 minutes.

3. Meanwhile, bring a large skillet with 2 inches of water to a simmer over medium heat. Add cider vinegar and season with salt. Break one egg at a time into a cup then tip cup into pan. Simmer until whites are set and yolks are soft but slightly set, about 3 minutes. With a slotted spatula, scoop out eggs one at a time and drain on paper towels. With a paring knife, trim edges.

4. Divide asparagus among four plates and drizzle with reduced balsamic. Top with shaved Parmesan and an egg.

Main Dishes

Vodka Pasta

(I found this in a great cookbook "Trattoria" by Patricia Wells.)

Ingredients:

1/4 cup olive oil

4 plump minced garlic gloves

1/2 teaspoon red pepper

Sea salt

One 28 oz. can tomatoes in juice

One pound penne

2 tablespoons vodka

1/2 cup heavy cream

1/2 cup snipped Italian Parsley

Directions:

Combine oil, garlic, pepper and salt and coat with oil. Cook over medium heat until garlic is gold, but not brown. Crush tomatoes into skillet. Simmer, uncovered about 15 minutes. Meanwhile in 6 quarts of boiling water, add 3 tablespoons salt and cook penne until al dente

Add pasta to tomato sauce. Toss. Add vodka. Toss. Add cream. Toss. Cover, reduce heat to low and let sit 1-2 minutes. Add parsley. Toss.

Chicken Scaloppini

2 eggs

1 cup breadcrumbs

Sea salt, Black Pepper, Lemon Wedges

Olive oil

2 whole chicken breasts, pounded to 1/4" thickness

Lightly beat the eggs in a shallow bowl. Season bread crumbs with salt (if they are homemade and not pre-seasoned). Pour enough olive oil into a skillet so it is 1/4" up the side of a large sauté pan. Heat until the oil is hot but not smoking.

Dip chicken breasts into the egg, let the excess drip back into the bowl and then dip into the breadcrumbs, shaking off the excess.

Sauté the breasts in bubbling, hot oil until they are golden on both sides (usually 4-5 minutes on each side)

Drain on paper towels. Salt and pepper each side generously while breasts are still warm and squeeze lots of lemon on them as you eat.

Pork Chops with Apples

1. Heat oven to 300 degrees

2. Brown pork chops (I use anywhere from 2 chops to 6)

3. Place around 3-4 peeled, cored and sliced apples in a greased baking dish.

4. Sprinkle with brown sugar and cinnamon. The recipe calls for 1/4 cup brown sugar and 1/2 teaspoon cinnamon, but I usually use more of both.

5. Dot with butter.

6. Top with browned pork chops.

7. Cook at least 90 minutes or until meat thermometer registers that pork chops are cooked throughout.

Sausage and White Bean Cassoulet

Ingredients:

- 4 sweet Italian sausage links (about 10 ounces total) skin pricked all over with a fork

- 1 teaspoon olive oil

- 2 medium onions, halved and sliced thin lengthwise (about 1 1/2 cups)

- 2 garlic cloves, chopped fine

- 1 1/2 teaspoon mixed chopped fresh herbs such as rosemary, thyme and or sage, or 3/4 teaspoon mixed dry herbs crumbled

- 1 bay leaf

- 1/2 cup chopped scallion greens or fresh parsley

- One 14 oz. can diced tomatoes with juice

- One 19 oz. can white beans such as cannellini, navy or great northern (or equal amount dried beans cooked) drained and rinsed

For topping

- 1 tablespoon olive oil

- 2 slices firm white bread diced (I use breadcrumbs)

- 1 small garlic clove, chopped fine

- 2 tablespoons finely chopped fresh parsley leaves

Directions:

In a medium skillet cook sausages in oil over moderate heat, turning them, until browned on all sides and cooked through (about 8 minutes.) Transfer to paper towels or something to drain

In fat remaining in skillet, cook onions and garlic, stirring until golden. Stir in herbs and bay leaf, scallions or parsley, tomatoes with juice and salt and pepper to taste. Boil mixture, stirring, 5 minutes. Cut sausage into 1/4 inch thick slices. Add sausage and beans to tomato mixture and cook, stirring until heated through. Discard bay leaf and keep Cassoulet warm, covered.

Make topping:

In a small skillet, heat oil over moderate high heat until hot (but not smoking) and sauté bread until pale golden. Stir in garlic, parsley, and salt and pepper to taste and sauté, stirring, one minute.

Transfer Cassoulet to a 1 quart serving dish and cover evenly with topping.

Pork Chops with Figs and Honey (from The Little Black Apron)

1/2 tablespoon olive oil

1 bone-in pork chop, trimmed of fat

Salt/pepper

2 tablespoons diced dried figs

1 teaspoon fresh thyme, chopped leaves only

1 teaspoon honey

1 teaspoon balsamic vinegar

1/3 cup chicken broth

1. Heat oven to 350 degrees

2. In an oven safe, 7" pan, heat olive oil on medium high. Once it is hot, season pork chops on both sides with salt and pepper and sear for 3 minutes until there is a golden crust. Then flip with tongs.

3. Put pan in oven for 5-7 minutes or until internal temperature is at least 145 degrees.

4. Remove pork chop from pan, cover and keep warm.

5. Put pan back on stove on medium high, wiping out excess grease. Add figs, thyme, honey, and broth. Boil. Then cook until reduced by 1/2. Season with salt and pepper. Spoon over pork chops and serve.

Super Fast and Easy Creamy Tomato Sauce

Ingredients:

2 tablespoons olive oil

1 onion, diced

1 clove garlic, minced

1 (14.5 ounce) can Italian-style diced tomatoes, undrained

1 tablespoon dried basil leaves

3/4 teaspoon white sugar

1/4 teaspoon dried oregano

1/4 teaspoon salt

1/8 teaspoon ground black pepper

1/2 cup heavy cream

1 tablespoon butter

Directions:

In a saucepan, sauté onion and garlic in olive oil over medium heat. Make sure it doesn't burn. Add tomatoes, basil, sugar, oregano, salt and pepper. Bring to boil and continue to boil 5 minutes or until most of the liquid evaporates. Remove from heat; stir in whipping cream and butter. Reduce heat and simmer 5 more minutes.

Roast

Ingredients:

1 (5 lb) eye of round roast

1/4 cup salad oil (I use olive oil)

2 tablespoons lemon-pepper seasoning

1/2 cup wine vinegar (I use red wine vinegar)

1/2 cup lemon juice

1/2 cup soy sauce

1/2 cup Worcestershire sauce

Directions:

Mix all ingredients and turn meat at least once a day for up to 3 days.

Cook, uncovered with marinade in Dutch oven at 250 degrees for 3 hours. Refrigerate overnight. (I serve hot that day).

Refrigerate overnight. Slice thin and serve with heated marinade.

Garnish with parsley and cherry tomatoes.

Also freezes well.

You can also take it about 30 minutes early, tent it with foil and then slice it for dinner.

Serve with Mashed Potato Casserole (follows).

Side Dishes

Mashed Potato Casserole

This is also a hit at every holiday dinner.

Ingredients:

8 large potatoes (I use about 16 and double the entire recipe)

8 oz cream cheese

1 cup sour cream

2 teaspoon garlic salt

1/2 teaspoon pepper

4 tablespoons butter

Directions:

Peel potatoes, cook until tender and then mash. (I just mix them in my kitchen aid blender.)

Beat cream cheese and sour cream together, and then beat into potatoes. Add garlic salt and pepper and mix thoroughly.

Pour mixture into a buttered, shallow 3-4 quart casserole. Dot with butter.

Serve immediately or you can cover and chill up to three days.

To reheat, bring to room temp, cover and bake in 400-degree

oven for 50-60 minutes.

Wrinkled Canary Potatoes with Mojo Rojo and Mojo Verde Sauces

Note: This is from Made in Spain by Jose Andres. I first saw this recipe on his cooking show. I used a blender, but would have used a food processor if I had one. Jose also INSISTED on his show that you crack open the small potatoes (I used fingerlings since I couldn't find potatoes from the Canary Islands!) and then put a dollop of BOTH sauces on it before popping it in your mouth! Now, I wouldn't eat it any other way.

Wrinkled Potatoes

Ingredients:

Serves 4

2 pounds baby potatoes

1 cup salt, plus more as needed

Mojo Rojo or mojo Verde, for dipping

Directions:

Place the potatoes in a deep, medium-size pot. Add enough water to cover, and salt. Potatoes should float in the salted water; if not, add more salt.

Place pot over high heat and bring to a boil. Immediately reduce heat to a simmer and cook until potatoes are easily pierced with the tip of paring knife, 25 to 30 minutes.

Drain water from pot, leaving just enough to cover the bottom. Return pot to low heat and cook, shaking pot until the salt covering the potatoes begins to crystallize, about 5 minutes. Remove from heat and cover pot with a clean kitchen towel until potato skins have wrinkled, about 10 minutes.

Serve immediately with dipping sauces, as desired.

Mojo Rojo

Ingredients:

Makes about 1/2 cup

8 cloves garlic, peeled

1 teaspoon sea salt

1 teaspoon cumin seeds

2 teaspoons sweet pimento (Spanish smoked paprika)

2 dried guindilla pepper, or other dried Chile pepper

1/2 cup Spanish extra-virgin olive oil

2 teaspoons sherry-wine vinegar

Directions:

Using a mortar and pestle, mash the garlic and salt to a smooth paste. Add cumin, pimento, and Chile pepper; mash until well combined. Slowly drizzle in olive oil while continuing to mash, until all the olive oil is absorbed. Turning the pestle in a slow, circular motion around the mortar, drizzle in 2 teaspoons water and vinegar. Keep at room temperature until ready to serve.

Mojo Verde

Ingredients:

Makes about 1/2 cup

6 cloves garlic, peeled

1 teaspoon sea salt

2 cups well-packed chopped cilantro leaves

1/2 teaspoon cumin seeds

1/2 cup Spanish extra-virgin olive oil

2 teaspoons sherry-wine vinegar

Directions:

Using a mortar and pestle, mash the garlic and salt to a smooth paste. Add cilantro leaves and cumin seeds; mash until well combined. Slowly drizzle in olive oil while continuing to mash, until all the olive oil is absorbed. Turning the pestle in a slow, circular motion around the mortar, drizzle in 2 teaspoons water and vinegar. Keep at room temperature until ready to serve.

Miscellaneous

No-Knead Bread (and story)

A few years ago, I began collecting recipes for no-knead bread. One recipe I cut out recommended the bread only is baked in a cast-iron Dutch oven so I saved the recipe for one day when I could afford my coveted orange Le Creuset Dutch oven (which, by the way, I still don't have).

Then, one day at the park I began talking about the recipe with a friend of mine from France, who is a fantastic baker. She told me she has had tremendous luck with the bread and loves to bring it to dinner parties as her contribution. During our conversation, I told her how I was waiting to buy the expensive French Dutch oven. She laughed. She told me she makes her bread in a Pyrex bowl with lid she bought at the supermarket. I laughed.

I went home and tried it in a Corning Ware dish with glass lid. It turned out fabulous. Then my parents bought me an inexpensive no-name Dutch oven. I baked the bread in it, it turned out fabulous.

I broke my Corning Ware dish and now just use the Dutch oven and a regular glass loaf pan to bake my bread. I usually make it 2-3 times a week. It is ridiculously simple and absolutely delicious.

Recipe: No-Knead Bread from the NY Times

Adapted from Jim Lahey, Sullivan Street Bakery

Time: About 1½ hours plus 14 to 20 hours' rising

3 cups all-purpose or bread flour, more for dusting

¼ teaspoon instant yeast

1¼ teaspoons salt

Cornmeal or wheat bran as needed.

1. In a large bowl combine flour, yeast and salt. Add 1 5/8 cups water, and stir until blended; dough will be shaggy and sticky. Cover bowl with plastic wrap. Let dough rest at least 12 hours, preferably about 18, at warm room temperature, about 70 degrees.

2. Dough is ready when its surface is dotted with bubbles. Lightly flour a work surface and place dough on it; sprinkle it with a little more flour and fold it over on itself once or twice. Cover loosely with plastic wrap and let rest about 15 minutes.

3. Using just enough flour to keep dough from sticking to work surface or to your fingers, gently and quickly shape dough into a ball. Generously coat a cotton towel (not terry cloth) with flour, wheat bran or cornmeal; put dough seam side down on towel and dust with more flour, bran or cornmeal. Cover with another cotton towel and let rise for about 2 hours. When it is ready, dough will be more than double in size and will not readily spring back when poked with a finger.

4. At least a half-hour before dough is ready, heat oven to 450 degrees. Put a 6- to 8-quart heavy covered pot (cast iron, enamel, Pyrex or ceramic) in oven as it heats. When dough is ready, carefully remove pot from oven. Slide your hand under towel and turn dough over into pot, seam side up; it may look like a mess, but that is O.K. Shake pan once or twice if dough is unevenly distributed; it will straighten out as it bakes. Cover with lid and bake 30 minutes, then remove lid and bake another 15 to 30 minutes, until loaf is beautifully browned. Cool on a rack.

Yield: One 1½-pound loaf. NOTE: DO NOT TELL ANYONE HOW EASY THIS IS!!! IT IMPRESSES PEOPLE EVERY TIME I MAKE IT. IT'S OUR LITTLE SECRET!

Brown Sugar Granola

Ingredients:

3 cups of old-fashioned oats

1 teaspoon cinnamon

½ teaspoon baking powder

½ teaspoon salt

½ cup of brown sugar

½ teaspoon vanilla

¼ cup of canola oil

2 egg whites

Directions:

Preheat oven to 350 degrees. Spray a jelly-roll or sheet pan with nonstick spray (or line with parchment paper, which is what I do).

In a mixing bowl, combine oats, cinnamon, baking powder, salt and sugar.

In a separate bowl, mix vanilla, oil and egg whites. Stir wet mixture into dry mixture and combine well.

Spread evenly on prepared pan. Bake for 30 minutes or longer, until well browned.

Let cool completely, and then break up with a spatula or by rolling up the parchment edges. Store in glass jars.

Salads

North African Carrot Salad from The Little Black Apron

Combine:

1 teaspoon olive oil

The juice of 1/2 a lemon

1/4 teaspoon of honey

1/4 teaspoon of ground cumin

Then pour over salad made of:

1/2 teaspoon chopped cilantro leaves

2 peeled carrots, cut on an angle

1 tablespoon golden raisins

Salt and pepper

My Favorite Salad with Honey Mustard Vinaigrette:

I got the vinaigrette recipe from Euro Chic, a blog sadly no longer around.

1 Romaine heart chopped (I know every cook in history says tear the leaves, but I always chop them and they seem to work just fine) If it is just my family I will use one heart, for larger family gatherings I will use 2-3 and double or even triple my vinaigrette recipe. (We usually have about 23 people for our get togethers). I rinse the leaves 3-4 times and spin them in my salad spinner — an indispensible object in my kitchen.

1-2 avocados chopped or even sometimes mashed. Sometimes when I toss my salad, if the avocado is really ripe and soft it just "mashes" onto the leaves and becomes part of salad.

Vinaigrette:

I take a Mason jar or Bonne Maman jar and put:

– 1 tablespoon Dijon on the bottom (I just use one of my soup spoons)

- 1 tablespoon honey (we buy this in bulk from Costco along with the olive oil there!)

- 1 chopped garlic clove

- 1 tablespoon white wine vinegar

- 3-4 tablespoons olive oil

Then I shake it and pour.

Basic Vinaigrette

Here is a basic Vinaigrette recipe chef Robert Arbor gives in his book "Joie de Vivre":

1 garlic clove

Salt, pepper

1 teaspoon Dijon

Red wine vinegar

Olive oil

He says to put the finely minced garlic clove in a bowl with a generous pinch of salt and 2 grindings of fresh ground pepper. Add mustard and vinegar (1-2 tablespoons). Mix and let sit while you wash the greens. Next, add oil (3 parts to one part vinegar). Stir constantly as you add the oil. Taste. Adjust seasonings.

Variations include adding: 2 teaspoons honey or juice of half a lemon or a splash of orange juice.

Lemon Vinaigrette on Greens

Another favorite. I am blessed to be part of a huge family who loves nothing more than getting together, so I am almost always the one asked to bring a salad. Here is another one that is a favorite at family gatherings.

1/4 cup lemon juice

1/4 cup vegetable oil

1/4 cup olive oil

2 green onions, finely chopped

1 tablespoon minced fresh Italian parsley

1 1/2 teaspoons sugar

1/2 teaspoon ground mustard

1/4 teaspoon salt

1/8 teaspoon pepper

Mix and pour onto: 4 cups torn romaine

Desserts

Biscotti

Ingredients

5 cups flour

4 teaspoons baking powder

1/2 teaspoon baking soda

1/2 teaspoon salt

1/2 cup butter, softened

2 cups sugar

6 eggs

1/2 teaspoon anise oil or 2 tablespoons anise extract

Sift flour, baking powder, soda and salt together three times. Set aside.

In medium bowl with electric mixer at medium speed, beat butter with sugar until very light, twenty minutes. Add eggs one at a time along with anise.

Add flour mixture, beat at low speed until blended. Divide mixture into four or six parts. Spread each portion on a greased and floured cookie sheet (or use parchment paper) and shape into 12 inch loaves. Bake in preheated 350-degree oven 15 to 20 minutes or until golden. Remove from oven. Cool 5 minutes. Cut into 3/4 inch thick slices. Turn each on its side and bake 5 to 10 minutes on each side until golden. Remove to wire rack and let cool.

Easy Cannoli

Here's what makes this easy: you buy packaged cannoli shells instead of making them, which usually involves a deep fryer. You can try to find them online or at Italian delis. I actually have a neighborhood Italian store that makes my shells fresh for me if I give them a few days notice.

Filling: Drain one, 32 oz. container of whole milk ricotta cheese in the refrigerator for one day by putting the cheese in a colander. Place a bowl underneath and cover with a towel. You want the cheese as dry as possible before you:

Mix with 1 ½ cups sifted powdered sugar, 2 teaspoons vanilla extract.

Combine and mix until smooth (about 10 minutes with an electric mixer). Optional: after mixing you can also stir in ¼ cup semi-sweet chocolate pieces if you like. (I prefer them without the chocolate.) Chill the filling in the refrigerator for at least an hour before stuffing shells.

CHAPTER 4

La Bella Casa

"Have nothing in your houses that you do not know to be useful or believe to be beautiful, " — William Morris, a British Craftsman, early Socialist, Designer and Poet, whose designs generated the Arts and Crafts Movement in England.

Yes, way, way before that popular book out right now about items sparking joy, Morris had it right.

The Italians are able to infuse art into everything they do and part of that is how they keep their homes. An Italian's home is a sacred space.

"*A ogni Uccello il suo nido e bello*" means basically "There is no place like home."

A typical Italian home is simple, but furnished with objects that have been carefully picked out for their beauty and usefulness.

A cluttered home may be found here and there in Italy, but more often, Italians keep their homes simple and neat. A typical Italian kitchen has as few objects on its counters as possible and usually sparkles with cleanliness. Italians take a lot of pride in keeping their homes as clean as possible.

Declutter

I think people in general have too much stuff and I believe that it weighs them down, physically and psychologically.

As I walk my children to school, I pass household after household that has its cars parked in the driveway because the garages are filled with stuff.

Any city or town boasts at least a dozen lots with storage spaces for people to store the extra junk that doesn't fit in the garage or attic or basement.

I think that belongings have energy and that having too much clutter weighs you down.

I am a minimalist so I frequently evaluate my "stuff" and donate, sell or trash items that are not adding to my life in a meaningful way.

Not long ago, I heard online about the "100 things" project where you take one month and rid your home of 100 items. This was a terrific exercise for me. It helped me look at what truly mattered, what I needed, what I loved and what I didn't. I sold some items online – an antique bathtub we had never installed, a window, girl's ballet shoes – and was able to start an emergency fund with the proceeds. My husband would like to be a packrat if left to his own devices and even he will tell you that he has not missed one item we sold for one second.

I recommend that anyone who wants to live a life in line with *la bella figura* should simplify their belongings to only keep what they love or find useful.

A fun website to check out if you are interested in decluttering your home is www.FlyLady.net. She has great tips on housecleaning and being organized as well as decluttering. One strategy she recommends is taking 15 minutes each day to declutter. She calls it "The 27-Fling Boogie."

It basically involves taking a trash bag and walking through your home and throwing away 27 items as fast as you can. Then take an empty box and collect 27 items to donate or give away.

Don't save your best

Another very *la bella figura* philosophy is to use what you love. This means that I took my great grandma's carnival glasses out of storage in the basement and put them in my cupboard front and center so they get used.

Am I worried about them breaking? A little. I have two small children, but it is worth taking the chance that one or two will break. To me, that is better than keeping them in a box in storage only to pass onto the next generation, who will keep them in a box in the attic or whatever. What is the point of that? Use and enjoy what you own.

I read that French women use their good cutlery and china every day. I don't know if this is true or not, but I like to believe it is.

One-trick ponies

I absolutely love Dan Ho (of the Discovery Channel) and his tips on keeping a clutter-free home and kitchen. My favorite tip from him is to make sure you aren't keeping any "one-trick ponies" around.

For instance, a garlic press is a one-trick pony because it only does one thing – press garlic.

Sometimes we find ourselves with too many specialty gadgets that just clutter our life and give us more work.

I had a George Foreman grill for a while. I used it every Sunday to grill my Italian sausages for my Big Sunday Dinner. After a few months I grew to despise that thing.

How can you hate an object, you might wonder? I did. It was a model that had the grill attached and you could not submerge the whole thing in water. So it would take me about 30 minutes to clean it and I would end up with a ruined dishrag and a big dripping, greasy mess on my counter each time.

It got to the point where I dreaded cleaning it and would let the thing sit on my counter dirty for three days until I got the gumption to tackle it. Now why on earth would I do this to myself? I still don't know, but one of the best days ever in my kitchen was when I threw that thing in the trash instead of trying to clean it again.

Now, I grill my sausage in my big cast iron skillet or if I'm worried about the extra grease, I will put it on a rack on top of a cookie sheet in my oven and bake them. Either way, I have an easy mess to clean up after.

So get rid of your garlic presses or any other "Albatross" disguised as a so-called "helpful" kitchen accouterment like my George Foreman grill. Get rid of the items that are more work than they are worth.

The Functional Kitchen

My kitchen simplification actually came about as a side effect of an impromptu kitchen remodel. I had a wall of hanging cabinets over a counter that separated my kitchen from my dining room. I would lean down and peek my head under the cabinets to talk to my kids at the table while I was working in the kitchen. It was absurd. So one day, I told my husband that with or without his help, I was ripping down the cabinets. He decided it would be better if he helped.

I lost about four cabinets this way. At first I put the items that had been in these cabinets in the basement and ran downstairs to grab what I needed.

Then I read "Joie De Vivre" by Robert Arbor and embarked upon the ultimate kitchen simplification project. Now, I don't know what I ever fit in all that extra space because what I have now works just fine.

Here's what Arbor writes are a few of the necessary objects in your kitchen:

What You Need

"It is not a good idea to purchase a lot of pots and pans and other equipment that you are not going to use," Arbor writes.

"There is no point in having every kind of cake accouterment if you never bake cakes . . . I always feel sorry for newlyweds who get overwhelmed with too much kitchen stuff that they have no idea how to use. It is better to give them one good copper pot that they will use forever than a set of highly specialized chef's knives that are just going to gather dust," he writes.

"A basic family kitchen only needs three or maybe four pots. These should be made of heavy-duty stainless steel and should have lids. To cook most meals, a set of small, medium, and large — the exact size will be determined by how many people are in your family — will do the trick," said Arbor. "The fourth pot can be an extra small pot for heating small amounts of milk, reheating leftovers, or poaching an egg. Or maybe you want a large pot — called a fait-tout — that holds about twelve quarts if you need to boil large amounts of pasta or make stock frequently."

Arbor said your basic pan supply should mirror your pot supply (get small, medium and large sizes with lids).

A basic kitchen should probably also include a "cocotte, a deep, oval casserole-type dish that can either go on the stove or in the oven. A cocotte, usually made of cast iron or enamel over cast iron, should have a heavy lid and is perfect for roasting a chicken, simmering a stew, or making a gratin."

Arbor also suggests that you really only need three knifes: a chef's knife, a bread knife and a paring knife.

CHAPTER 5

How to Act Chic

This next section is basically a small primer on how to act chic.

It is something I work on constantly and sometimes my efforts

fail.

For instance, I think it is NOT chic to swear and used to

include this as a tip to acting chic, but I've given up. I too

often revert to this language for emphasis. I blame it on

working in a newsroom where profanity flies constantly.

Here are some tips for acting chicly and maintaining or

creating *la bella figura*.

* Have impeccable posture. This takes pounds off your frame

and can do more than anything else to improve the way

people perceive you. Good posture equals self confidence and

self confidence is the most attractive trait you can have. Read

"Your Carriage, Madam" by Janet Lane.

* Learn to walk slowly and gracefully.

* Maintain your mystique. You don't need to elaborate when someone compliments you. A simple, genuine "thank you" will suffice.

* Don't talk about yourself so much. Be well read and well informed so you always have something interesting to add to a conversation. Talk about books you are reading, films you have seen, recipes you like and so on. But try not to talk about yourself or other people. Besides, it's boring to talk about yourself anyway! There is something my mother once told me that you would do well to remember: "Great minds discuss ideas, average minds discuss events, small minds discuss people."

* Think before you react, act or speak. Try to practice your tone and volume. I'm Italian-American and this is a constant struggle for me. I get too passionate, too loud and too shrill sometimes. Some of the time is okay. All of the time is not.

* Prioritize your time. Make sure you are dedicating the majority of your time to the things that are most important in your world. If your children are the most important, make sure you are not spending all your time keeping a clean house when you could be playing with them.

* Prioritize your money. Are you spending your money in line with your priorities, values and passions?

* Eye contact. Eye contact. Eye contact. Period.

* Develop an attitude of nonchalance. Now that I am "of a certain age" I am really trying to work on a nonchalant attitude about so many things in my life. I expend the energy when it is necessary, but it is so freeing just to let some things go. I used to get into heated discussions with some family members who didn't see eye-to-eye with me. But I don't anymore. An uber chic online friend summed it up once by saying, "It's a bore to try to explain why you do something to people who will never understand."

- Be smart. Jamie Cat Callan wrote in "French Women Don't Sleep Alone" that smart is sexy and she's so right. Don't be afraid to use big words and talk about big ideas. Keep abreast of current affairs.

- Become bilingual. Speaking more than one language is also super sexy.

CHAPTER 6

Your Inner Italian Girl

This is something I have read about in several places,

including Anne Barone's "Chic and Slim" books and by

reading Debra Ollivier's fabulous, must-have book, "Entre

Nous".

This exercise involves writing a profile of your alter ego. It is

about crafting your future persona, the person you wish to be,

the person inside you waiting to emerge. It helps to read this

"profile" or "portrait" often as a reminder of who you want to

be.

The following portrait is my Inner Italian Girl. As you read,

keep in mind that some of it is reality, some fantasy, some

dreams, but ideally it should sum up this entire book ….

Meet My Inner Italian Girl, Gabriella:

Gabriella luxuriously cups her hand around her warm cafe au lait bowl, taking sips in between bites of her homemade bread, toasted and buttered. Around 10, she will have an espresso, black, to tide off her hunger until her noon lunch. For summer lunches she will eat a salad and during the winter — a bowl of soup — with a small piece of bread and sliver of gourmet cheese.

For dinner she will eat pasta, chicken or fish with a vegetable and salad, along with a glass of wine. She usually reserves desserts for Sundays.

On Sundays, she refrains from spending any money. She spends the day going to mass and then to the "after party" at her mother-in-laws house and then home to an early, big Sunday supper, usually around 3 or 4.

During the warmer months, meals are eaten en tavola, al fresco, at the picnic table on her patio. A colorful tablecloth is complimented by big terra cotta pots of red geraniums bordering the patio.

Do this

Nearby, tomatoes, rosemary, basil and Italian parsley grow in a row of pots, along with potted lettuces and other greens.

For larger feasts and gatherings, another long table is brought outside and placed end to end with the picnic table and spare wooden chairs are brought outside.

As the sun sets, a string of colorful bulbs hanging from a row of small trees are turned on. Small white lights are woven through the gazebo and a few lanterns dangle from tree branches.

Gabriella fills her life with intellectual, emotional and spiritual pursuits; spending her free time focused on books, film, food, good conversation and good friends. She strives to live a life rich in experiences and not things.

Her passions are her family, reading, writing, hanging out in cafes, playing chess, studying foreign languages, taking photos and making art, especially religious Mexican style art.

Her closet reflects her minimalist aesthetic. It is neat and simple. Her palette of colors is limited to the perennial fashion colors: black, navy, gray, ivory along with a smattering of turquoise.

She owns a small, but perfect-fitting wardrobe. Every item is of the highest quality she can afford and works with her body, style and life. She buys new items rarely and with much thought. She resists impulse buys, preferring to save her money for a truly long-term fashion investment *SAKS* or travel to one of her favorite vacation spots: New York, Italy, France, San Francisco or Spain. *Fatima Hawaii*

When she does buy something it is from a list of clothing items she needs to replace or feels will be an important addition to her wardrobe. She will also spend time hunting down the best bargain.

If she doesn't feel a resounding YES when she tries on an item, she will not buy it. On her list right now are soft winter cardigans, a pair of walking boots for winter and sexy, feminine, unique tops like the ones worn by Audrey Tatou in "Priceless" and by Julie Delpy in "Before Sunset."

Once she takes a clothing item or accessory home, she babies it. She line-dries her tee-shirts and hand washes all her lingerie. Like chic European women, she will not buy something unless she has cash. That means avoiding a credit card except for emergencies. She carefully saves for her purchases and will do without something until she can afford the best quality version.

Now that she is "of a certain age" she knows quality counts even more. She will, however sometimes bargain shop for accessories, such as her favorite scarf, trendy sandals and black beads (all from Target).

She tends to spend more money on haircuts and classic shoes. She only owns a handful of shoes that she cares for meticulously. She also only owns three handbags: two high quality designer bags (one in black, one in navy) and a vintage black patent leather pocketbook for dressy occasions.

Her pantry is slim. She doesn't buy in bulk unless it is during her quarterly trip to a warehouse store where she will stock up on olive oil, Parmigiano Reggiano, coffee and dried pasta from Italy. Otherwise, she shops two to three times a week, filling her French market basket mostly with fresh produce. She never snacks and always sits to eat. She always puts her utensils down between her small bites. She chews slowly, savoring all the flavors.

Her kitchen is small and meticulously kept clean and free of clutter, like the rest of her home. In fact, everything in her home is either beautiful or useful. She lives by the William Morris adage that "Have nothing in your house that you do not know to be useful or believe to be beautiful."

The decor theme in her home revolves around unique, mostly original artwork, lots of books, plants and big comfy furniture with sumptuous fabrics and soft, sparkling lighting. She has a few treasured items displayed that are meaningful to her, but her real joy lies in her bookshelves, where she keeps only well-loved volumes. DONATE?

She frequents the library often, riding her bicycle there and piling books into her metal basket. She will stop at the thrift store nearby and scan for bargains like the vintage black cocktail dress she once found there. It is easy to shop at a second-hand store because her finite palette of wardrobe colors limits her gaze.

After a year of careful spending and saving, her credit cards and car are paid off. Her savings account is healthy and besides a mortgage, she is debt free. She saves all year for her annual vacation.

Her older model sedan is lovingly maintained and she has no desire to spend her hard-earned money on a newer version as long as her car continues to get her from point A to point B. She would rather save her money for something that is an "experience" instead of a new "thing."

She uses a strict household organizational chart that allows her to keep a tidy home using a minimum of her precious time. She would rather spend that time reading, daydreaming or conversing at a cafe. By tackling one area of her house everyday she keeps it presentable. A basic sweeping of the dining room and kitchen is done every night after dinner and every morning after the children leave for school, she sweeps the entire house.

She does not hurry because she believes that caring for your possessions increases the appreciation you have for everything in your life. She is also frugally chic and hangs her laundry to dry, uses cloth napkins and natural cleaning products like vinegar in her home. She enjoys old-fashioned domestic arts such as baking your own bread and using cast iron skillets to reheat something instead of using the microwave.

She has developed an aura of mystique, refraining from sharing details of her life with acquaintances. She tries not to talk about herself, but instead talks about ideas. She can intelligently discuss the latest local, national or international news or a new book or film she has seen. She is very passionate, but is able to share her opinions in a poised manner.

She has impeccable posture and maintains her weight plus or minus 3 pounds.

She does not worry anymore. *Holy* She is assertive. She can respond to requests by saying, "No, I'm sorry I can't do that," or "I'm sorry I don't attend (home sales parties), but thank you for asking," without feeling the need to explain or defend herself. She also does not elaborate on a compliment but simply says a gracious "thank you."

She is a devoted walker and walks or bikes to the library, market, coffee shop, her children's schools, the wine store, etc. She also is a staunch defender of the 9 hours of sleep she requires every night.

Every day she makes sure to count her blessings and appreciate her life right then and there.

ADDITIONAL THOUGHTS

1.   Make a list of the things that are most important in

your life. *dating for finding a good kind loving supportive Husband*

2.   Identify your top 5 values. For me they are family,

health, independence, creativity and spirituality. Make sure

the majority of your wealth and time is directed toward

enhancing these five values. For instance, I don't mind

spending extra money on organic food because both health

and my children are in my top five values.

3.   Make a list of a handful of material objects that enhance

your life and make it rich and meaningful: those few objects

you really don't want to live without. *Books music* For instance, my list

would include my laptop, my camera, my books and a few

other items. Notice how many things you own that don't

make this list.

JO photos

Relics, 2 shoes socks food Bible water filter

4.   Another way to do this is to list the material objects you

own that would make it into your car if you had an hour to

gather belongings before a fire swept through your

neighborhood. My list includes photos, heirloom quilts, my

camera, art work and some important documents.

5.   List the simple pleasures you enjoy in your life or wish

you had time to enjoy. Take the time to recognize and

Art Music Writing Singing

appreciate the small things in life.

6.   Make a list of what you are grateful for and review it

often.

7.   Remind yourself that being stylish does not take

money.

8.   Always pick quality over quantity, whether it is your

clothing, the number of friends you have or the food you eat.

9.   Play up your strengths. Do you have perfect

cheekbones, great legs or hair to die for? Emphasize them in

your style choices.

10.   Don't feel guilty spending time and effort to look your best. It enhances your self-esteem and lets you present your best self to the world so you can stop worrying about how you look and concentrate on other things. Also, by taking the time to look your best, you are showing that you respect yourself and others.

11.   Never look like you tried too hard. Try to perfect the technique of looking as if you just casually threw your outfit together. Nonchalance.

12.   Learn a handful of age-old Italian beauty secrets, such as using olive oil on your skin and on your hair.

13.   Give sleep the importance it deserves. Take it from Sophia Loren: getting adequate sleep is one of the most important things you can do for your health and your looks. Don't skimp on it.

14.   Remember that self-confidence is the number one thing you can work on to be more attractive.

15. Only buy what you love. Don't buy something to just "make do." Only buy something that really speaks to you, whether it is a set of pasta bowls or a pair of leather gloves. Be picky. Find what you love or go without.

16. Acquire and maintain a sense of mystery about you, especially as you get older. As Veronique Vienne says, "Replace youth with mystery."

17. Be interested. It makes you interesting. Constantly learn and be curious about life.

18. Don't be afraid to show your intelligence. Also, don't be afraid to admit your ignorance on certain subjects.

19. Be spontaneous. Do something unexpected, adventurous.

20. Declutter your closet as well as your kitchen. You don't need a big kitchen or expensive items to be a good cook.

21.   Pursue your passions. Take a page out of Jackie O's book. Don't give your passions short shrift. Make sure you dedicate meaningful time to what you love. Jackie looked at her passions as a lifelong love affair.

22.   If you are single or married, make time to be alone. Appreciate your own company.

23.   Realize that there is nobody else in the world just like you. Everyone has flaws or character defects just like you do. Love yourself and then you can truly love others.

24.   Discard things or objects in your life that take up your valuable time without providing the same amount of worth (for instance, my George Foreman grill).

25.   Study and read books on food. Watch "Food, Inc." Read Michael Pollan.

26.   Sign up for a Community Supported Agriculture share or shop at the Farmer's Market. Remember that you are what you eat.

27.　Move your body. Walk or ride your bike whenever you can. Remember that physical exercise can be made part of your daily life and doesn't have to involve joining a gym, unless you are into that sort of thing.

28.　Keep a bowl of fresh fruit on your counter or kitchen counter. It is beautiful and good for you!

29.　Make at least one meal a ritualistic, meaningful part of your day. Take your time. Savor your food.

30.　Eat food you love or nothing at all. Be a food snob.

31.　Try not to look at shopping or cooking as a chore. Look at it as a labor of love, a way to love your body, your family and yourself.

32.　Start your own Big Family Dinner tradition. If you don't have a large family or live alone, get a group of friends together and make this a tradition.

About the Author

Kristi Belcamino is a crime fiction writer, cops beat reporter, and Italian mama who also bakes a tasty biscotti. In her former life, as an award-winning crime reporter at newspapers in California, she flew over Big Sur in an FA-18 jet with the Blue Angels, raced a Dodge Viper at Laguna Seca, watched autopsies, and conversed with serial killers.

She is the author of the Gabriella Giovanni mystery series (HarperCollins). https://www.amazon.com/Kristi-Belcamino/e/B00GN8C6SC/ The first book in the series, *Blessed are the Dead*, based on her dealings with a serial killer, was nominated for the 2015 Anthony and Macavity awards for best first novel. The third series book, *Blessed are Those Who Weep*, was nominated for the 2016 Barry Award for best paperback original. Here is what Lisa Unger said about it:

"*Blessed are Those Who Weep* is a crackling, emotional, and rocket-paced mystery. Kristi Belcamino brings her reporter chops to Gabriella Giovanni, the very best kind of heroine -- smart, plucky, and true. Keep your eye on this writer."

Kristi's first young adult mystery, *City of Angels*, (Polis Books) will be published in 2017. Her nonfiction writing has appeared in several publications, including the New York Times, Salon, Writer's Digest, Miami Herald, Chicago Tribune, and the San Jose Mercury News. Kristi now works part-time as a police reporter at the St. Paul Pioneer Press. She lives in Minneapolis with her husband and her two fierce daughters.

Find out more at http://www.kristibelcamino.com. Find her on Facebook at https://www.facebook.com/kristibelcaminowriter/ or on Twitter @KristiBelcamino. Sign up for her newsletter here http://www.kristibelcamino.com/contact/newsletter/

how to act chic: have impeccable posture. This
will do more than anything else to improve the way
people perceive you. good posture equals self
confidence and self confidence is the most attractive
trait you can have.   Your carriage modern by
Janet Kone. Learn to walk slowly + gracefully.
— dont talk about yourself so much. Be well red and
well informed so you always have something interesting
to add to a conversation. Talk about Books you are
reading, films you have seen recipes you like
Try not to talk about yourself or other people. It's
boring to talk about yourself; my mother told
me: "Great minds discuss ideas, average minds
discuss events, small minds discuss people".
Think before you act = act or speak.
write letters to John-Owens. prioritize your money.
Are you spending money on your priorities, Values,
  passions? (* opera dress + dress shoes   Eye contact
Eye contact. Eye contact. Period. so freeing to just
let some things go at this age. It's a bore to
explain things to people who will never
understand. dont be afraid to talk about
  big ideas or use big words
- By tackling 1 area of her house everyday she keeps it neat.
sweep the diningroom + kitchen every night after dinner
and every morning, sweep the house.

book: chic + slim   Impeccable posture + maintain
    Entre Nous   wait up or down 3 pounds

Say no and thank you for inviting me without explaining
or defending yourself. a staunch defender of
her 9 Hours of sleep she needs+ makes a grade Pride
list of things every day.
work on self confidence the #1 thing you can do
to be more attractive, and your daily posture.

Camping   Chanel bag

- {3/4 Camel coat single breasted tie

{ or Reefer + Camel pants + Camel

{ turtle neck - cashmere or cotton

(Louis Vitton Bag
Paul yermon
Necklace + Ring)

- custom jeans to balance greatly different legsizes. which
style? What material?
black jeans for dressier look

- cultivate scarves for class - best style?
Black + Beige beautiful Bras + a few Xlnt
Colorful Bras, the best I can buy

custom
Trashy Lingerie Bras Xlnt fit wear like iron
white nude black pink turquoise purple
Lavender eyelet stretchy Red magenta

- Take small bites. chew thoroughly. Savor each bite
in this way get more satisfaction. I realize I am
satisfied sooner. only eat food you love. If it
doesn't taste awesome, don't eat it. Keep portions
Small. learn what a portion size is and stick to
that. meat = deck of cards or your palm
walk daily during the summer months. no snacking
Michael Pollans food rules: eat food, not too much,
mostly plants. (#2) "dont eat anything your great-
grandmother wouldn't recognize as food." (3) dont
eat anything with more than 5 ingredients or ingredients
you cant pronounce. stay out of the middle of the
grocery. shop on the outer aisles. (4) dont eat anything
that wont rot, ie twinkies (5) Its not just what you
eat, but how you eat. stop eating before you are full.
avoid processed foods and foods with high fructose
corn syrup. It costs more but is part of living
"Bella   figura"

Made in the USA
Lexington, KY
06 January 2017

make a pantry list of perishable +
nonperishable + keep on Refrigerator
make copies + circle what you need.

Comaflogel problem areas: upper arms throat bust stomach theighs' bottom? well, I guess I cant see it, so its not a problem just needs to fit in clothes. Bod feet

good areas: forearms, lower legs, feet, hands nose

spend my money on tommy tuch, breast reduction left, lipo etc stomach, thighs, flab under arms
(or) if not "S.d.c.s." spanks or girdle with long cover for theighs, xlnt bras fitting but looser Bra for underarm flab.

have a repstore of recipes in 3 ring binder. Keep Recipes to try in pocket of folder meat, poltry, misc w. bread, desserts, vinagretts, vegetables.
Sunday dinner: protein, fresh Baked Bread, veg. dessert
Monday: (Soup) (salad) leftovers
Tues: leftovers or Eggs + Toast (Crumpets)
Wed: Pasta w/o Red Sauce
Thurs chicken winter: Roasted chicken
Freday
sat: pork chops Romaine lettuce Avocado Honey mustard Dressing

have nothing in your house that is not useful or beautiful. donate sell or trash items not adding to my life
www.flylady.net DAN to Discovery channel for Clutter free House + Kitchen

read Chapter 6 / Exersize *** reserve dessert for special occasions

develope an aura of mistigue, talk about books, shows, ideas ·Be intrested. It makes you intresting. move your body at ads,

What readers say ...

"Have you wished you could capture that elusive quality that makes Europeans, well, so European? If you wish you could find a handbook with European recipes for living, look no further! La Bella Figura will show you how. From simplifying your closet to setting your table, this little book will do it all. Weaving her European sensibility with practical advice, (Belcamino) shares her secrets to crafting a life that is rich in experiences. Imbued with her Italian heritage and a love of European lifestyle, this author gives meaning to the Italian philosophy of la bella figura. Bravissimo!"
- My French Corner.com

"La Bella Figura is a lovely book that offers up prac~~~~~~ ~~~ refining (or even creating) a simple and stylish l~~~~ books challenges the accepted ideology of 'more, ~ favor of luxurious frugality and pursuing your t~ Heartily recommended to xenophiles and simpl~~~

About Author Kristi Belcamino

Kristi Belcamino is a crime fiction writer, cops beat reporter, and Italian mama who also bakes a tasty biscotti. In her former life, as an award-winning crime reporter at newspapers in California, she flew over Big Sur in an FA-18 jet with the Blue Angels, raced a Dodge Viper at Laguna Seca, watched autopsies, and conversed with serial killers.

She is the author of several books including the Gabriella Giovanni mystery series (HarperCollins). The first book in the series, Blessed are the Dead, based on her dealings with a serial killer, was nominated for the 2015 Anthony and Macavity awards for best first novel. The third series book, Blessed are Those Who Weep, was nominated for the 2016 Barry Award for best paperback original.

Her nonfiction writing has appeared in several publications, including the New York Times, Salon, Writer's Digest, Miami Herald, Chicago Tribune, and the San Jose Mercury News. Kristi now works part-time as a police reporter at the St. Paul Pioneer Press. She lives in Minneapolis with her husband and her two fierce daughters.

Find out more at http://www.kristibelcamino.com.
Facebook: https://www.facebook.com/kristibelcaminowriter/
Newsletter: http://www.kristibelcamino.com/contact/newsletter/
Twitter: @KristiBelcamino

ISBN 9781540649478

90000 >

9 781540 649478